Promise and Possibility

Hope-Filled Devotions

By Tracy Hill

ISBN: 978-0-9976913-2-0

Dedication

To Grandpa and Grandma Leavitt, for sharing with me the
hope of Jesus.

Introduction

In the person of Jesus, hope is already ours, but we must daily and purposefully choose to embrace it. Often it goes against the feelings, circumstances, and difficulties we inevitably face. Hope is deliberately choosing—despite all else— to open the shutters each morning with Jesus on our mind and a contented smile in our heart, knowing that no matter the weather, come rain or shine, it's all going to be OK. Hope is swinging the front door open wide to greet the day, remembering God's promises and seeing possibility in all that comes our way. Hope that is sure, steady, and true is based not on ourselves, others, or our situation; it is based only on Jesus and all that He has done, all that He is doing, and all that He will continue to do in our lives.

Hope is waking up with the knowledge that you and I, and the day belong to the providential care of our loving and powerful LORD.

Jeremiah 29:11, "'For I know the plans I have for you,' declares the LORD, 'plans to prosper you and not to harm you, plans to give you hope and a future.'"

Hello, Hope

Take a moment and don't delay,

introduce yourself to the *hope* found in Jesus,

just say *hello* and invite it to stay.

Even if you need to reintroduce yourself day after day,

stick at it and bit by bit,

hope will settle in,

making its home in your heart

where it will finally remain.

Romans 15:13, "May the God of hope fill you with all joy and peace

as you trust in Him, so that you may overflow with hope by the

power of the Holy Spirit."

Covered

As I walked through the park this glorious morning, a wooden structure in the middle of the grass caught my attention. Upon closer investigation, I noticed it was sheltering a fragile little sprout. Someone had obviously placed this makeshift fortress here to guard and protect the fledgling tree from harm, giving it a chance to establish roots and reach maturity. Immediately I saw a parallel between the tree, and God and me. As God's children, we are all covered with His love and protected by His sturdy strength. Under His attentive care, we can sink our roots deep into the Savior and gain nourishment from the countless promises revealed in His Word. Covered in God's love, we're able to grow and mature and flourish into all that He has planned. We're covered from our first moment of belief until Jesus returns or calls us home. And on that day seeing Him face-to-face, we'll finally reach our full maturity and stand before Him in perfect completion.

Covered under the care of God's watchful eye is where our growth occurs. It's where we not only survive, but also where we fully and abundantly thrive.

Psalm 52:8, "But I am like an olive tree flourishing in the house of God; I trust in God's unfailing love for ever and ever."

Psalm 91:4, "He will cover you with His feathers, and under His wings you will find refuge; His faithfulness will be your shield and rampart."

Glorious Hope

The burden of perfection, the pressure of getting it right, is lifted from our shoulders as we place our faith in Jesus Christ. It is through Him alone that we are justified—declared and made right—in the eyes of God. His sacrifice was the payment for our sin. He lovingly covers our shame. The door that was previously closed is now swung graciously open. The access to God we were once denied is replaced instead with an extended invitation. In faith, we approach Him; by His grace, He accepts us. In His Presence, we experience His magnificent glory. The hope to end all hopes is actually just the beginning.

Romans 5:1-2, "Therefore, since we have been justified through faith, we have peace with God through our Lord Jesus Christ, ² through whom we have gained access by faith into this grace in which we now stand. And we boast in the hope of the glory of God."

Onward Hope

Some days it feels as though we're jumping over hurdles and weaving through obstacles—everything is a struggle. Sometimes it's not just a day like this, it may be a week, a month, a season. During times like these, the hope of climbing into bed and pulling the covers over our heads at night sounds like just what we need and is the motivation that keeps us moving forward. But, there is a hope much more compelling and rewarding than this. It's the hope of eternity with our King, and the hope of Jesus with us each day, in every situation. We have the hope of growing in character as we learn to respond to trials in a way that pleases the Lord. As God's beloved children we are meant not to just endure, but to triumphantly persevere. We can cling to the assured and confident hope of being victorious in Christ. God has given us His Holy Spirit which inspires us to press on, by continuously reminding us of the love God has for us. Love on which our hope firmly rests. His love is the ultimate hope that calls us onward.

Romans 5:3-5, "Not only so, but we also glory in our sufferings, because we know that suffering produces perseverance; [4] perseverance, character; and character, hope. [5] And hope does not put us to shame, because God's love has been poured out into our hearts through the Holy Spirit, who has been given to us."

At Its Fullest

My life is found when I lay it down. Instead of clutching it tightly to my chest, I unfold my arms and give myself to You. At the foot of the Cross, my hope is found. As I lay my life down, giving it over to You, I am free to receive the new life You have for me—a life that seeks Jesus over self.

A life of self is fruitless and void. A life full of Jesus is gloriously satisfying; it is rich and abundant.

A life full of self is an endless pursuit of greed and want. A life in Christ is a passionate quest of love and gratifying sacrifice.

A life full of Christ is life at its fullest. A life full of Christ is to the glory of God.

Luke 9:23, "Then He said to them all: 'Whoever wants to be My disciple must deny themselves and take up their cross daily and follow Me.'"

Every Petal

As a child, you may have picked a daisy and played a wistful game of chance. As you plucked the petals one by one you would alternate saying, "He loves me, he loves me not," always hoping to land on an affirmation of love. With God, every petal pulled is an assured, "He loves me." His love for us never fluctuates. His love doesn't depend on our ability or performance. His love is the same whether we deserve it or not, on any given day. His love doesn't depend on our lovability; He just loves.

Psalm 33:22, "May Your unfailing love be with us, LORD, even as we put our hope in You."

Fullness

I long to live in the fullness of Your Presence. Your love. Your peace. I come to You Lord, to receive the fullness of life, to be washed in the richness of Your grace. In You, I am made complete. The fullness of Your love is what my heart has searched for, and I am satisfied. Amen.

Psalm 63:5, "I will be fully satisfied as with the richest of foods; with singing lips, my mouth will praise You."

Ensuring Safety

As I walked along the dirt path, two birds with long spindly legs ran over to my right side. As I glanced to my left, I noticed three baby birds running off in the opposite direction. My first thought was that these two larger birds—apparently, the mother and father—had abandoned their little ones, leaving them all alone to fend for themselves. I quickly realized they left their children for a good purpose—they were keeping their eye on me and escorting danger far away from their vulnerable children. As soon as Mama and Papa Bird made sure I was at a safe distance from their cherished tots, they turned their attention from me and quickly ran back to their kids. As I reflected in awe of this precious sight, I was reminded of the loving, protective care that our Heavenly Father has for us. The times we feel all alone and abandoned, left to fend for ourselves, just may be the moments God is escorting danger away from our path. He goes before us, and drives evil away, clearing a path of safety for us, His beloved children.

Proverbs 2:8, "for He guards the course of the just and protects the way of His faithful ones."

Amen

Lord, help me to keep my eyes on You,

My mind steady on Your Word,

My ears attuned to Your Voice,

My heart anchored to Your Spirit. Amen.

Deuteronomy 30:20, "and that you may love the LORD your God, listen to His voice, and hold fast to Him."

Raise Your Banner

A life surrendered to Jesus is not a white flag of defeat but rather a glorious banner of victory. Defeat comes when we give up on everything, but victory is declared the moment we surrender it all—our life, plans, purpose, and circumstances—over to the Lord.

By joining ranks with the Lord, we are guaranteed victory. He is the One leading the charge of our defense; He has conquered death on our behalf; He continually defeats the sin that seeks to destroy us; He faces our enemy head on; He overcomes on our behalf. God is faithful to deliver us.

Tear up your white flag of defeat and raise your banner of victory! Give thanks to the Lord and find hope in Him, in all things.

Psalm 20:5, "May we shout for joy over your victory and lift up our banners in the name of our God. May the LORD grant all your requests."

1 Corinthians 15:57, "But thanks be to God! He gives us the victory through our Lord Jesus Christ."

Fireflies

As of this writing, I have only seen fireflies once—though it is a memory that sticks with me. Surprise and delight overtook me the moment I first witnessed this tiny bit of *spectacular* dance through the air. I clearly understood why children chased after these little sparks of light, hoping to capture one for themselves. Holding this small glow of brilliance in the cup of one's hands elicits both giggling joy and wide-eyed wonder. Something about this special light brought a joyful lift to my heart that night.

The heavenly nature of light appeals to our senses; it captures our attention, peaks our curiosity, and draws us in. Light stands in sharp contrast to dark, shining all the more brightly when held against the blackness of night. Jesus has told us that He, Himself is the light of the world—a light that never fades, dims, or dulls. Unlike the firefly whose light shines for but a brief season, His light radiates brilliantly, all year round, for all of eternity.

In His light, there is blessed fellowship with Him. In His Presence, sparks of peace, hope, and joy catch fire in our hearts, igniting a blaze of light in our lives.

John 8:12, "When Jesus spoke again to the people, He said, 'I am the light of the world. Whoever follows Me will never walk in darkness, but will have the light of life.'"

Above

We have two mindsets from which to choose—yes, there are just two. We can choose to focus solely on all that immediately surrounds us, or we can lift our eyes to heaven and see the world through the broad lens of eternity. Each vision brings with it a perspective unique in its view. Focusing only on earth and all that it holds reveals a small scope of limitations, binding us to the "here and now" with little hope on the horizon. By raising our sights and setting our hearts on Jesus, and on the things *above*, our lives become filled with hope of exponential potential, of all that can possibly be. Eyes just on the *world* can bring feelings of ever-searching emptiness. Eyes on *above* ushers deep abiding joy, peace, contentment, and hope. *Above* motivates our thinking, passions, pursuits, actions, and dreams with fresh enthusiasm, purpose, and means. *Above* is where our hope is found, with the heavenly purpose of bringing hope into the world all around.

Colossians 3:1-2, "Since, then, you have been raised with Christ, set your hearts on things above, where Christ is, seated at the right hand of God. ² Set your minds on things above, not on earthly things."

Not Disappointed

Many people and things become the focus of our hope. We grow to depend on them much more than we should, more than God intended. After all, people are fallible and things wear out. As much as we'd rather not admit it, and as hard as we might try, there comes a day when the person we've made our object of hope won't measure up to our need and will ultimately let us down. The things we've purchased and heaped our hope onto will bend, break, and just plain old wear out. None of these hopes, no matter how good, will ever be as sure a hope as Jesus.

If you're looking for a hope that will never disappoint, look no further: Jesus is your answer. He is the hope God planned for you from before the foundation of the world. Place your daily and eternal hope in Him. You will not be disappointed.

Romans 5:5, "Now hope does not disappoint, because the love of God has been poured out in our hearts by the Holy Spirit who was given to us." NKJV

Endless Supply

God doesn't dispense His love one sprinkle at a time. He scoops it out and pours it on with lavish and abundant generosity. There is never a shortage of love for His children; there's enough to go around. God's loves never runs out. He has an endless supply.

Deuteronomy 5:10, "But showing love to a thousand generations of those who love Me and keep My commandments."

Sweetest Rest

Lord, You calm my mind and ease my fears. When rest seems elusive, I turn my thoughts to You. I am gently reminded of Your faithfulness, power, and love. Sleep that before was fretful is now the sweetest rest.

Proverbs 3:24, "When you lie down, you will not be afraid; when you lie down, your sleep will be sweet."

Fly

"What if I fall?

Oh, but my darling

What if you fly?"

Recently at a barnyard-style flea market, an old wooden sign caught my eye—it had the above saying painted sweetly across. My heart skipped a beat when I read these words. They are words inspiring faith in possibility. They are words expressing hope in the promise of what could lie ahead if we just have the faith to step out and try. By overcoming our fears and reaching out beyond the horizon, we come to a place where amazing things happen. We have the option of keeping our feet firmly planted in the comfort and safety of what we know, or we can step out of the familiar into the wild blue yonder where life is vibrant and bold and takes our breath away. Jesus earnestly calls for us to step out in faith and hold onto Him all the way. If by chance we fall, He is right there to catch us. And if we indeed fly, He will undoubtedly soar with us to unimaginable new heights. Either way, He's present with us. Whether we fall or fly, we've stepped out in faith. There is no failure in faith or belief, or trying. If we never try, we'll never know all that's possible. So let's give God our fear, stretch our wings wide, and step out in faith and fly.

James 2:22, "You see that his faith and his actions were working together, and his faith was made complete by what he did."

Nectarine Promise

Each year I witness the changing of seasons through the life cycle of the nectarine tree growing in my backyard (also pictured on the cover of this little book you're holding). Each winter the tree stands stark and bare, the bark is brown, and the limbs are leafless. Surprisingly at the start of each spring, the seemingly dead tree emerges alive as tiny pale pink buds begin to sprout and then slowly unfurl into blossoms of life. As the months of springtime tip toe along, the tree fills in with an abundance of green leaves, and what used to be blossoms now hold the promising beginnings of delicious fruit. The little greenish balls which cling to the branches quickly grow into an abundant harvest of ripe nectarines—they flourish faster than I can harvest them, and the sheer number is more than my family can eat.

Summer, the next season in the repeating cycle, is when all the fruit has been picked and is gone from the tree, but the leaves are still green, and life is very evident. The months move along, and the waning of the summer sun means the crispness of autumn is not too far off. Autumn is the season when the leaves start to fall and the tree prepares for another hibernation. Then once again, the cold winter arrives, and the seemingly lifeless tree is back to bare.

Though the tree appears dead, hidden from our eyes there is vibrant life running through its veins. The harshest of seasons cannot steal what's inside. The tree is just hunkering down for the winter, storing up strength for its next season of blooms.

And then the whole cycle goes around again.

The same can be said of us: our lives are a continuous cycle of a series of ups and downs. When we face seasons of harsh environments we're wise to seek hibernation with the Lord, where despite the bitter cold, His life continues flowing through our spiritual veins, sustaining and nourishing our souls. And when seasons of warmth and sunshine once again follow, our lives bud and flourish, testifying to the vibrant, enduring life of Christ in us.

Knowing the One who holds the seasons of nature and of my life in His hands gives me indescribable comfort and optimistic hope in the promise of His plans. In His perfect timing, God follows winter with the fruit of spring.

Ecclesiastes 3:1, "There is a time for everything, and a season for

every activity under the heavens..."

All

Jesus wants you for more than a couple of hours each Sunday morning. He wants more than weekend visits. He wants to do *all* of your life with you, *all* of the time. He's the lover of your soul. He desires more than anything to be by your side, moment-by-moment, in good times and bad. He came from Heaven to be your lifelong partner; He laid down His life, and gave His *all* for you. Don't miss out on His blessings. Give Him *all* of you.

1 John 3:16, "This is how we know what love is: Jesus Christ laid down His life for us."

He Knows

God knows your heart because He is the One who formed it. He knows what motivates and encourages you, what deters and discourages you. He understands your emotions and thoughts, your actions and reactions. He knows and understands it all. You are never a surprise to God. He is the only One who knows your truest self—the parts no one else perceives. He sees beneath the surface, straight into the recesses of your heart, and He lovingly and graciously considers it all.

Psalm 33:14-15, *"from His dwelling place He watches*

all who live on earth—

[15] He who forms the hearts of all,

who considers everything they do."

God Acts

God notices.

God cares.

God intervenes.

God rescues.

God loves.

God acts.

Isaiah 64:4, "Since ancient times no one has heard, no ear has perceived, no eye has seen any God besides you, who acts on behalf of those who wait for Him."

Hand it Over

If we allow it, the pain from rejection will steal our blessings of abundant peace, hope, and joy. These blessings will be hijacked right out from under us if we're not careful. The experience of rejection can cause us to be hyper-vigilant in guarding our hearts, but that becomes so tiresome and lonely. God knows our heart, even the innermost parts, and He would very much like to guard it for us.

If you've ever struggled with rejection (who hasn't at some point), then here's a prayer for you:

Lord, help me to surrender the hurt of my rejection to You—the rejections of the past, and present. Help me to surrender the rejections of the future that haven't yet occurred, but still manage to hold me captive in fearful expectation. Help me to surrender every last bit of the rejection I feel over to Your care. I want to live in freedom. I don't want to be afraid to offer my heart, and I don't want fear to hold me in bondage any longer. Please Lord Jesus, help me to hand over the pain of my rejection, so I can experience Your healing, live renewed in confidence, and receive the fullness of Your blessings. Amen.

Psalm 62:8, "Trust in Him at all times, you people; pour out your hearts to Him, for God is our refuge."

Grow Deep

Jesus is our Source of Life; He is our Living Water. Plant our life in Him, sink our roots down deep, and we will never wither. The drought may come, the rain may cease, but He remains our Well-Spring forever. Sink our roots down deep by investing time in precious prayer, communicating with our Sovereign God. Grow deep by opening our Bible and pulling out treasures of Truth to claim for ourselves, and by surrounding ourselves with sisters-in-Christ, our precious companions. Sink our roots deep, in season and out. Our leaves will remain green and abundant, vigorous and strong when we grow deep. Fruit will blossom on our branches as a testimony to our Savior, as a banner for the Lord. He is our sustainer, our reviver, our strength, and our song.

Let your roots grow deep into Jesus all year long.

Jeremiah 17:8, "They will be like a tree planted by the water that sends out its roots by the stream. It does not fear when heat comes; its leaves are always green. It has no worries in a year of drought and never fails to bear fruit."

Healing Words

As a child, you may have heard or even spoken the words, "sticks and stones can break my bones, but names will never hurt me." Those words are just a tough façade covering over a broken heart. I'm sure you have realized the power words possess to either inflict injury or bring healing. At some point, you've most likely either spewed ugly words delivering pain, or have been on the receiving end. Words spoken in anger, frustration, and jealousy often cause a bitter sting and a lasting scar. Perhaps there are words that still haunt you, labels you can't seem to shake. Let me take a moment to speak healing to you right now. Whatever words you've heard thus far, they needn't have further hold over you. God's words are the ones that ring eternally true. He says you are beloved, chosen, forgiven, and beautiful. You are His child, you are worth dying for, you are worth pursuing, you matter, you have purpose, and you are special.

You my dear, are loved beyond measure. You are His. Moving forward, let these truths be the basis of your identity. Hold your head high. You are a daughter of the King, and that makes you royalty.

Song of Songs 4:7, "You are altogether beautiful, my darling; there is no flaw in you."

Clean

I am clean.

I am purified by Jesus.

I am baptized in the Spirit.

I am washed through the Word.

Yes indeed, I am clean.

1 Corinthians 6:11, "But you were washed, you were sanctified, you were justified in the name of the Lord Jesus Christ and by the Spirit of our God."

Restored

As I drive along the coast each winter, I can't help but notice the shoreline disappear; where towels once lay in the warm honey sand, there is now a sheer drop-off to water below. Each year, the pounding surf eats at the coastline grain by grain, and during a storm surge, large scoops are carried away at once. It always seems an impossible feat that the shore could be restored in time for the next summer season, but year after year, the sand that disappeared is miraculously returned. The granules that had been carried out to sea, tossed and turned, sifted and refined, are graciously returned to the stability of land. Year after year the same cycle repeats itself—the ebb and flow of the tide, the push and pull of the waves slowly erode the beach, and then just as slowly restore the sand to the place from which it was taken.

During the moments or seasons when you're caught in the turbulence, and it feels as though everything is being stripped away, choose to remember that God is still God and He's always at work. It may be a season racked with tossing and turning, but in that time God is quite possibly doing some sifting and refining of His own, in you. Trust in God; keep your hope in Him. In His perfect timing, He will faithfully restore you.

Psalm 80:3, "Restore us, O God; make Your face shine on us, that we may be saved."

I Can

Bear with me through a few negative sentences, as I'll then use them to share a positive message.

I can never get past my failures.

I can never forgive those who hurt me.

I can never get through this situation.

I can never overcome my fears.

These are all lies we too often believe. They are lies that hold us captive. They are lies that render us powerless. They are lies that keep us from the abundant life that God has in store.

I'd like you to take a pen—a red marker if you have one—and go back over the previous statements of "I can never," and boldly cross out the "never" in each one.

Now reread each statement through the eyes of God, mindful of His power at work in you.

I can get past my failures.

I can forgive those who hurt me.

I can get through this situation.

I can overcome my fears.

God makes the impossible into something quite astonishingly possible.

Philippians 4:13, "I can do all this through [Christ] who gives me strength."

Perhaps you have your own "I can never" statement in mind; I'd like you to write it out and cross through the "never" with a huge 'X' mark. Now read it aloud with confidence. This is your new statement. Claim it as your own.

Write your statement here:

Windows Down

I thoroughly enjoy driving with the car windows down. The sun shines in to warm my body. The breeze flows through my hair and I don't even care that it gets messed up. It rushes past my face, bringing an exhilarating feel of refreshment. All my senses come alive when the great outdoors invade my space.

As strange as this may sound, my life with Jesus is a lot like driving with the windows down. My life with Jesus is tangible, bigger, vast, and open. With Jesus in my life I come alive, all the way from the top of my head to the tips of my toes. He opens my eyes, awakens my spirit, and refreshes my soul. He invades my heart and sets me free.

Psalm 23:3, "He refreshes my soul. He guides me along the right paths for His name's sake."

Complete Surrender

Whether it's time for a rededication of your life or an initial surrender, God wants you—all of you. He seeks a revival in your heart. If you let Him, He will give you a new life and a fresh beginning from this day forward. In your surrender, you will find forgiveness and freedom. You will find your place of belonging. You will discover your value and worth. You will find meaning. Listen and obey the voice of Jesus calling your name. Listen and obey the voice within your own heart that yearns to surrender it all to Him. Give in to surrender.

Complete surrender cries, "Here's my heart Lord. It's all Yours."

Psalm 84:2, "My soul yearns, even faints, for the courts of the LORD; my heart and my flesh cry out for the living God."

Until the Day

Even though snails move at an extremely slow pace, they do seem to progress towards their final destination. Sometimes I feel like a snail—though I'm heading in the right direction, it feels like I'm getting nowhere fast. If I had my way, I'd be perfect right now. I really want to say the right things, do the right things, and think the right things. I want to be more like Jesus. So, to speed up the process, I lean on Him; I walk with Him; I seek Him; I talk to Him; I listen to Him more and more. Sometimes I feel I should be reaching my destination of perfection much quicker than I am and get frustrated with myself for being so slow, but God is so graciously patient with me. He knows I'll never be perfect this side of eternity. It's simply not going to happen until Jesus comes back or He calls me home. God just wants me to keep heading in the right direction, to stick with the process, and day by day He'll perfect me a little more. Then in one glorious moment, it will happen, I'll see Jesus face-to-face and I'll finally be flawless in every way. So I'll keep pressing on, until that day.

Philippians 1:6, "being confident of this, that He who began a good work in you will carry it on to completion until the day of Christ Jesus."

Galoshes of Joy

When my kids were young they played outside daily, including the rainy days when most people stayed dry inside. I remember one afternoon when we donned our galoshes and buttoned our raincoats and braved the wet stuff falling from the sky. Besides running around and stomping in puddles, the boys bravely skateboarded (seated on their bottoms) down the slope of the driveway, ending with a splash as they rolled through the flowing gutter. They made the best of that rainy day. The wet droplets did nothing to stifle their joy.

Likewise, we have the choice: let problems of life overwhelm us and dampen our day, or put our galoshes on, choose joy, look for opportunity, and dance in the rain.

Psalm 30:11, "You turned my wailing into dancing; You removed my sackcloth and clothed me with joy."

Straight Through

Occasionally the Good Lord takes us not around the storm, but straight through it. Sometimes, an atmospheric disturbance is called for, to shake us up and refocus our minds and hearts onto Him. He uses the storm to whittle away our pride and self-reliance. When the rains pour down and the winds howl past, as life swirls about, our need for Jesus becomes increasingly clear. And when the storm has passed and we have a moment to catch our breath, God will show us—if we let Him— how such horrible turbulence was used to accomplish His good purpose in us.

While enduring the storm, we usually don't conceive how any good can come of it, but hindsight often gives us a better view. Looking back with God's perspective, we're given comfort as we realize He never left our side. Looking back, we also see His hand at work, refining and perfecting us, making us into His beautiful reflection. You see, His greater purpose is not for our earthly ease, but for our heavenly growth. God has a plan and it's always for our good.

The next time a storm hits and Jesus takes you straight through, let go of yourself and hold tight to His hand. Trust His purpose; trust His goodness; absolutely, trust His love.

Romans 8:28-29, "And we know that in all things God works for the good of those who love Him, who have been called according to His purpose. ²⁹ For those God foreknew He also predestined to be conformed to the image of His Son, that He might be the firstborn among many brothers and sisters."

Glimpses

Hope is like...

Catching glimpses of blue

In a storm-filled sky.

We must raise our heads,

Lift our eyes,

Look up toward the heavens to find them.

Hope is like...

Catching glimpses of God

In a trial-filled moment.

We must raise our heads,

Lift our eyes,

Look up toward the heavens and we will find Him.

Psalm 42:5, "Why, my soul, are you downcast? Why so disturbed within me? Put your hope in God, for I will yet praise Him, my Savior and my God."

Wildflowers

This season, the wildflowers seem to be going completely wild. They are growing everywhere, climbing mountains, filling valleys, thriving in gutters, and springing from cliffs.

They are surviving, succeeding, growing, and blossoming in every possible environment. Despite the fact they weren't planted in a luxurious meadow, they are flourishing right where they are. The most beautiful thing about these wildflowers is their resilient ability to grow anywhere. Spotting them in unsuspecting, even difficult places is half the pleasure.

Are you like the wildflower blooming where God has you planted? Or are you waiting for Him to first uproot and replant you into a more perfect and pleasing terrain?

Nothing brings Jesus more pleasure or glory than when despite your circumstances, you grow for Him and become His beautiful display. I encourage you to bloom like the wildflower at this very moment, right where you're planted, even if it feels like you're down in the gutter or dangling from a cliff. Despite your current situation, get rooted in Jesus and flourish in Him.

Psalm 92:12-13, "The righteous will flourish like a palm tree, they will grow like a cedar of Lebanon; ¹³ planted in the house of the LORD, they will flourish in the courts of our God."

Your Voice

Wherever my feet lead me, I hope it is only where the Lord has gone before. Any time I veer in one direction or another, I pray it is only because the Lord has clearly spoken, "this is the way to go." May I never venture anywhere without my Companion, my faithful Walking Partner. Only the Lord truly knows the best route for me to take; may I always heed His instructions and value His directions.

Lord, help me to hear Your voice above every other; may Yours ring out loud and clear. Even if it's spoken with the gentleness of a whisper, may I hear and faithfully obey. Amen.

Isaiah 30:21, "Whether you turn to the right or to the left, your ears will hear a voice behind you, saying, 'This is the way; walk in it.'"

And God Said...

Smile.

I love you.

Count your blessings and you'll feel better.

You have a lot to be thankful for.

Psalm 21:6, "Surely you have granted him unending blessings and made him glad with the joy of Your Presence."

Come Alive

If we're not careful, our faith can become dead as dry bones. Left unattended, unnurtured, and uncultivated, our faith quickly turns lifeless and unfulfilling. Without a continual fresh filling of the Holy Spirit, our spiritual life can become stale instead of vibrant. Faith is meant to be a relationship in which we walk hand-in-hand with Jesus, alive in His Spirit. The Lord intends for our faith to be dynamic, with our hearts on fire for Him. With the help of the Holy Spirit, it can be. Although we are forever secure and sealed with the Holy Spirit, as children of God we need an extra-large dose and fresh filling every day. Ask Him to pour out and overflow His Spirit in you. Ask Him to fill you up to the tippy top. Scripture says to ask and it will be given. The Father delights in giving His Spirit to those He loves.

Ask Him to breathe life into your spiritual bones. It's time to come alive!

Ezekiel 37:3-5, "He asked me, 'Son of man, can these bones live?' I said, 'Sovereign LORD, You alone know.' ⁴Then He said to me, 'Prophesy to these bones and say to them, "Dry bones, hear the word of the LORD! ⁵This is what the Sovereign LORD says to these bones: I will make breath enter you, and you will come to life."'"

Completely Spent

When we find our energies completely spent, all attempts to fill ourselves fully exhausted, it is then that we find God. When we finally come to the end of ourselves and our wild attempts, after searching everywhere for fulfillment, we arrive at the realization that nothing apart from Christ will so perfectly suffice. Our hearts will continue in dissatisfaction until we find our rest in Him. Cry out to Jesus now and be satisfied.

God, Himself is completely spent on our behalf. He gave His Son, He gave His life, He gave His all. He sacrificed everything to win us back, to draw us into His extended, welcoming arms.

1 John 4:9, "This is how God showed His love among us: He sent His one and only Son into the world that we might live through Him."

Discerning the Best

Lord, help me to discern not only between bad and good, but also between better and best. Help me to live my life not according to my own flawed standard but by the righteous standard of Christ. Please lead me in Your perfect way, so that someday I might stand before You pure and confidently blameless. Amen.

Philippians 1:9-11, "And this is my prayer: that your love may abound more and more in knowledge and depth of insight, ¹⁰ so that you may be able to discern what is best and may be pure and blameless for the day of Christ," filled with the fruit of righteousness that comes through Jesus Christ—to the glory and praise of God."

Gentle Nudges

Lord, help me to trust and submit to Your ways. Help me to heed Your gentle nudges that point me in the right direction, and obey the promptings of Your Spirit. Let the path You lay before me always lead me straight to You.

Proverbs 3:5-6, "Trust in the LORD with all your heart and lean not on your own understanding; [6] in all your ways submit to Him and He will make your paths straight."

Blessed Unity

Father, Son, and Spirit—a perfect Union of Three in One, The Holy Trinity.

By the Father's plan, through the Son's sacrifice, and of the Spirit who is poured out and breathed in us, we too are brought into fellowship, sharing intimacy, joining in the Blessed Unity forever and ever. Amen.

Acts 2:38-39, "Peter replied, 'Repent and be baptized, every one of you, in the name of Jesus Christ for the forgiveness of your sins. And you will receive the gift of the Holy Spirit. [39] The promise is for you and your children and for all who are far off—for all whom the Lord our God will call.'"

Holy Dwelling

Redemption is to take the old and make it new, to take the broken and make it whole, to take the dead and give it life. In Jesus, our lives are redeemed. As redeemed people, we no longer wander aimlessly searching for a home. He's laid out a welcome mat inviting us to take up residence with Him, in His holy dwelling. When our heart becomes His, His home becomes ours.

Exodus 15:13, "In Your unfailing love You will lead the people You have redeemed. In Your strength, You will guide them to Your holy dwelling."

Spring Forward

Year after year, the arrival of spring is acknowledged in the setting of our clocks and watches. We set them to spring forward one hour, allowing for extra daylight at the end of our day. Is this extra hour for cramming in more stuff that needs to be done? Or is it a lovely opportunity to do something we enjoy? Something as simple as watching the sunset, marveling at the colors as they swirl in the sky, taking an evening stroll to inhale the fresh air, or heading out to the backyard to enjoy the glad birdsong of nightfall.

Lord, help me to make the most of the blessed gift of time, even if that means doing less. Amen.

Ecclesiastes 3:11, "He has made everything beautiful in its time. He has also set eternity in the human heart; yet no one can fathom what God has done from beginning to end."

Easter in My Heart

Many years ago, my Grandma gave me a set of little, white coffee mugs with pastel-colored hearts painted all around. On the front is a painting of a young girl with pigtails in her hair and a cheerful smile on her face. Her hands are folded in front of her chest as she kneels before the Lord in prayer. Written in black, child-like font are the words, "Dear Lord, help me keep Easter in my heart all year." These mugs are a reminder of a simple and powerful truth. Jesus died to bring us hope and joy not just for one day a year, but for all the days of our life.

The most important and life-changing thing we could ever know is the devoted and sacrificial love of Jesus. He endured the Cross for our sake. His death brought us salvation and His resurrection brought us eternal life. Because of Easter we also have the promise of a new and abundant life here and now. Easter is meant to impact every area of our lives as we see everything through a fresh, hope-filled perspective of Jesus.

Let's gratefully reflect on the sacrifice of the Savior and celebrate Easter in our hearts every day.

John 19:28-30, "Later, knowing that everything had now been finished, and so that Scripture would be fulfilled, Jesus said, 'I am thirsty.' A jar of wine vinegar was there, so they soaked a sponge in it, put the sponge on a stalk of the hyssop plant, and lifted it to Jesus' lips. When He had received the drink, Jesus said, 'It is finished.' With that, He bowed His head and gave up His spirit."

May Day Blessings

When I was a young girl, around age eight or nine, I had a special way of celebrating the first day of May. I'm not sure how I thought of this, or where I learned to celebrate this day—the only thing I can think of is possibly from a book of nursery rhymes my Grandma used to read me. But on this occasion, I made special May Day baskets for my neighbors. I arranged hand-picked flowers into little bouquets, placed them in homemade baskets of construction paper and ribbons, set them on front porches, and then rang the bell and ran away to hide. I would peek out from my hiding place to witness unsuspecting neighbors open their door to a delightful May Day surprise. Their blessing tickled me with joy.

Wouldn't it be wonderful if, as adults, we engaged in such whimsical blessings towards one another? Wouldn't the world be a brighter place if not just on May Day, but every day of the year, we went out of our way to do something kind for no other reason than to just be kind, with no thought of reward or acknowledgment, but blessing in secret, just for the sake of blessing? Let's make it our secret mission to surprise someone with kindness and love today.

1 John 3:11, "For this is the message you heard from the beginning: We should love one another."

Get Guidance

Far too often, we rush off ahead of Jesus and suffer the consequences of our haste. Day by day, moment by moment, there are decisions both big and small we constantly face. Jesus highly recommends that we first pause and seek His wisdom and expert advice. He knows what dangers and pitfalls lurk up ahead, but also where the unexpected pleasures and hidden treasures can be found that we might otherwise miss. When you get that urge to hurry on your way, first stop, take a breath, seek the Lord, and wait and listen for His voice. Then proceed according to His sovereign way.

When you seek His guidance, He is always faithful to divulge His will.

Proverbs 1:5, "let the wise listen and add to their learning, and let the discerning get guidance."

In the Word

Far too often I have spoken without enough thought. Far too often, I've wished I could put my words back in my mouth, but unfortunately that's impossible. I can tell when my time in the Bible has been less than it should; not only is my mind impacted, but my words follow suit. I have found that the more time I spend in the Word of God, the more blessed my own words become. They tend to linger on my tongue with the sweetness of love and honey instead of sour bitterness and regret. The more I'm in God's Word, the kinder my own words sound, the truer my own words ring, the more blessing I pass on, and the less shame I'm left to feel. The more time I spend in the Word of God, the more my own words become like His.

Psalm 119:11, "I have hidden Your word in my heart that I might not sin against You."

Psalm 19:14, "May these words of my mouth and this meditation of my heart be pleasing in Your sight, LORD, my Rock and my Redeemer."

Fire-Proof Faith

Daniel 3:16-18, "Shadrach, Meshach and Abednego replied to him, 'King Nebuchadnezzar, we do not need to defend ourselves before you in this matter. [17] If we are thrown into the blazing furnace, the God we serve is able to deliver us from it, and He will deliver us from Your Majesty's hand. [18] But even if He does not, we want you to know, Your Majesty, that we will not serve your gods or worship the image of gold you have set up.'"

The three young men whose story is found in the book of Daniel are the ultimate examples of fireproof faith. They were put to the test and passed with flying colors. Faced with a literal life-or-death situation, these men refused to bow down to fear and give it any authority or power over their lives. They resolved to trust their God and cling to the hope He provides. They were able to stand strong in their convictions and conquer their fears because whether they lived or died, their lives were in His hands. They knew the trustworthy, loving character of God, and they believed His promises according to Scripture to be true for themselves.

As you read further in their story, you will see they walked in freedom even in a blazing furnace; the ties that were meant to bind fell off, releasing their hold on them. Miraculously, a fourth Figure was seen walking amongst the flames along with these men—undoubtedly, it was their Mighty Savior who never left their side. Though the scorching flames burned even onlookers, these men emerged from the fire unscathed. Their confident hope and unwavering faith were an undeniable testimony to everyone present and all who heard their story.

Lord, whether the fiery flames merely lick at my heels, or completely pin me in, I pray to be like these hope-filled men and stand firm in You, unwavering in my faith. Help me to stand strong against fear, trust in You, and hold onto Your promises. Even when hardships press in and it feels like I'm surrounded by fire, I pray that I continue to walk in the freedom that You purchased for me. May my life be a testimony to the hope, glory, and power of the One True God. Amen.

Entire Being

Ears- Listen and hear the Gospel Message of Jesus.

Mind- Be open to and truly understand the hope it holds.

Heart- Believe it to be true and receive if for yourself.

Mouth- Confess that Jesus is your personal Lord and Savior.

Feet- Act on what you believe and confess. Let it change your life.

Faith involves our entire being. Faith doesn't stop at hearing about Jesus; it doesn't end with understanding who He is. These mark the beginning of our unfolding faith. Jesus calls us to a faith that goes much deeper than mere knowledge in our minds. For faith to hold any significance in our lives, it must move beyond the surface and the superficial, and invade the deepest recesses of our hearts. We must truly believe that Jesus is Lord and Savior and receive Him as our own. Faith must be invited to settle in and make our heart its home. Faith brings with it the blessings of hope, peace, and strength, and gives rise to an uncontainable joy that compels our mouths to shout from the rooftops, "Jesus is my Savior, Jesus is my Lord." But we can't stop there. Let's make sure we put feet to our faith. Action is the evidence of what our heart believes. Scripture even admonishes that faith without action is dead. Real faith is alive, it calls us to live and breathe and follow Jesus with everything we've got.

Salvation is just the beginning of our faith. Faith is an ongoing journey that involves our whole being.

Romans 10:9-10, "Because, if you confess with your mouth that Jesus is Lord and believe in your heart that God raised Him from the dead, you will be saved.[10] For with the heart one believes and is justified, and with the mouth one confesses and is saved." ESV

Faith

Faith is not something that just happens, but rather something we choose daily, moment-by-moment. We choose to believe what we cannot see. We believe in God's promises and hold them to be true. We set our hearts firmly upon them to see us safely through. Faith is something intangible we know to be real. Faith is the shelter where we seek refuge from the storms raging all around, and the uncertainty we feel. Faith is within reach and an option for all—we just need to grab it, embrace it, and never let go. Faith is a choice that transports us above earthly constraints and into the heavenly, supernatural Presence of God. Faith is seeing possibility from His point of view.

Hebrews 11:1-3, "Now faith is confidence in what we hope for and assurance about what we do not see. ² This is what the ancients were commended for. ³ By faith we understand that the universe was formed at God's command, so that what is seen was not made out of what was visible."

In His Hands

This topsy-turvy world is full of unpredictable uncertainty, and despite our best efforts and well laid plans, we don't really know exactly what each day will hold. When chaos comes creeping in, there's no need to despair. Remember, we know the One who calls light out of darkness and holds our day in His Hands.

The key to our hope is not in what the day holds, but in He who holds the day.

Psalm 24:1, "The earth is the LORD's, and everything in it, the world, and all who live in it; ² for He founded it on the seas and established it on the waters."

Gatherings and Collections

Through the years, I've had quite an array of collections, of which included a case full of Barbie dolls and all the associated accessories and clothing. I've gathered a container full of rocks—the shapes and textures ranging from smooth and shiny to rough and rugged, with varying colors of brown, black, white, and even a few brilliantly colored ones. I've had a shoebox filled with Pez dispensers and little packets of candy that were inserted inside. Each one had a different cartoon character head on top. Over the years, I acquired a collection of record albums, including everything from my early-childhood songs, to my more grown-up teenage interests. As a young girl, one of my finest collections was that of small, clear-plastic animals, each accented with bright touches of paint. Every time I went to the market with my Grandma, for the price of a quarter, she would purchase an animal figurine for me from the vending machine as we exited the store. In my mind, these little figures were priceless, as if they were made of real crystal.

These varying collections were my prized possessions; I would take them out periodically and admire them as the treasures they were. Over the years, I have lost track of many of these childhood collections, but the memories stick in my mind.

As I have grown older, I have developed a new interest and have begun a new collection: words from the pages of the Bible that seem written just for me. As I pore over Scripture, I quite often come across a verse that speaks directly to my heart and feeds my very soul. They are these that I gather as personal messages from God, tucking them safely and securely into my heart and mind. I take them out often and admire their beauty. I am always adding to my glorious collection. Word-by-word, phrase-by-phrase, I gather more and more. I will never outgrow or tire of this collection; in fact, my passion only deepens. I hope to pass this collection on to others as an inheritance—an inheritance of much more value and worth than any earthly possession I could possibly gather.

Isaiah 57:13, "When you cry out for help, let your collection of idols save you! The wind will carry all of them off, a mere breath will blow them away. But whoever takes refuge in Me will inherit the land and possess My holy mountain."

Lavish

The love of Jesus is both shockingly scandalous, and extravagantly lavish. His love goes where most avoid. His love does what no other will.

His love for us is quite scandalous: He loved us despite our sin; He pursued us in spite of our past. He loved us enough to pull us out of the depths and into His arms.

His love for us is remarkably lavish: By His blood, He saved us from our sins. Through His sacrifice, He rescued us from ourselves. In His nakedness, He clothed us in His righteousness. He poured out His life for the sake of His love.

John 15:13, "Greater love has no one than this: to lay down one's life for one's friends."

Cool Breezes

Whenever I walk around my neighborhood on a warm afternoon and the cool breeze blows past, I can't help but think of Jesus. I'm immediately reminded of His love which refreshes and invigorates my very soul. I love the touch of the breeze as it flows over my body. Sometimes, I even throw my arms out to the side just to capture more of the caress. The breezes remind me of His love, swirling all around me, and as they float past, it's as if His gentle kiss is brushing against my cheek.

Psalm 63:3, "Because Your love is better than life, my lips will glorify You."

Humble Display of Greatness

When I think of Florence, Italy, numerous images come to mind:

The sight of children with outstretched arms, joyfully chasing pigeons in an innocent game of pursuit.

The sound of horse hooves clomping on the cobblestone as carriages full of curious tourists pass by.

Glimpses of people both young and old escaping the midday sun to enjoy a scoop of refreshing gelato in the cool shade.

The smell of leather goods wafting onto the streets from the doorways of many shops.

Of these vivid memories I recall of this distant, beautiful city, one stands out as most significant of all. It was an unexpected encounter that brought tears to my eyes.

Our journey this day was not planned, but rather we wandered wherever the path took us. Our feet led us to a quiet, out-of-the-way piazza (courtyard). It seemed to be an undiscovered treasure, hidden from the touristy crowd. My husband and I leisurely sat beside a fountain for a few moments until a non-descript church standing at the end of the square caught our eye and beckoned us over. As we entered this little church, the reverence and respect it drew was almost palpable, as the few of us visitors inside didn't utter a word. We quietly explored the various and gloriously understated rooms within, until turning a corner we found ourselves standing at the feet of Jesus. Right before our eyes, in this cathedral which had looked so plain from the exterior, was the near life-size, wooden carving of the Crucifix, by none other than Michelangelo. This sculpture was created long ago in 1492, yet to this day perfectly presents the message of The Cross.

There were no crowds around, there was no line to get in, and here I found myself standing before one of the most remarkable pieces of artwork in the world. Standing in the presence of this grand display—Jesus declaring His love for me, by giving His life for mine—the company of others around me faded into the background. I became overwhelmed, feeling the weight of the guilt, scorn, and shame that Jesus took from me. Tears of gratitude began filling my eyes. I stood in awe. This most humble of all the churches we'd discovered held the greatest treasure of all. This seemingly insignificant church was the perfect picture of who Jesus is—a Humble Display of Greatness!

I've since come to learn, this precious church is called the Basilica di Santa Spirito of Florence, meaning Church of the Holy Spirit. Yes, The Spirit was in that place, and I felt His Presence. He revealed to me my sin, my need, my surrender, my gratitude. He revealed to me my Savior, His love, His sacrifice, His mercy, His humility, and His greatness.

Psalm 38:4, "My guilt has overwhelmed me like a burden too heavy to bear."

Isaiah 53:5, "But He was pierced for our transgressions, He was crushed for our iniquities; the punishment that brought us peace was on Him, and by His wounds we are healed."

In Response

My sister is an elementary school teacher working with the primary grades, and in years past she was assigned to a school in a lower-income neighborhood. Each year I try to visit her classroom to watch her teach, to meet her kids, and to enjoy the special treat of reading them a book as the *mystery reader*. Sometimes I bring a favorite book from home, and other times I pick one from the class library. I get a kick out of it, and the kids seem to enjoy it too. Besides reading a book and helping with assignments during my visit, I also like to bring care packages containing various school supplies. I know that money is tight and funds are limited with many of the families, so I like to give each child a few items of their very own to keep at school or take home, whichever they prefer. One year I got everyone a pencil/supply box and filled it with colored pencils, regular pencils, stickers, markers, erasers, a sharpener, and various other items. They were delighted with their gift and so extremely grateful. They shared with me many words of thanks.

One little girl in particular stands out in my mind. Out of gratitude for the gifts I had bought her, she gave me a gift in response. She stood by my side, opened her itty-bitty hand, and revealed a tiny, teddy bear shaped eraser of her own. She ever-so-sweetly told me she wanted me to have it and placed it in my hands. I was overcome by her generosity, knowing that her gift was of great sacrifice. She gave it to me not out of plenty, but out of poverty and want. At first, I was hesitant to take it from her, knowing she didn't have a lot, but seeing what joy it brought her to give it to me, I eventually conceded. I still have that teddy bear eraser as a reminder of her precious sacrificial response.

This sentimental story is a reminder of what it means to accept the gift of salvation that Jesus bought for me. He didn't buy it in a store, He paid for it with His life on the Cross at Calvary. The price was too high for me to ever afford, so He paid it on my behalf. He ransomed me from the holds of sin and death, buying me a place in heaven eternally. Because He paid my debt, I am gratefully indebted to Him. In response and out of gratitude, as small as it may seem in comparison to the gift He purchased for me, I now place my life in His hands; I offer all of me. I give Him my thanks, my heart, my devotion. I gladly give Him all I have.

And He graciously receives my tender, child-like offering.

Mark 12:41-43, "Jesus sat down opposite the place where the offerings were put and watched the crowd putting their money into the temple treasury. Many rich people threw in large amounts. [42] But a poor widow came and put in two very small copper coins, worth only a few cents. [43] Calling His disciples to Him, Jesus said, 'Truly I tell you, this poor widow has put more into the treasury than all the others.'"

Humbly Fall

As a seed must first fall to the ground before taking root and blossoming into all it was designed to be, so too must we fall to the ground in order to become all that we were created to be. We fall to the ground in desperate need of the Savior; we fall to the ground in complete surrender to our Lord; we fall to the ground in reverent worship of our God. And as we fall, God is there to lift us up. He lifts us up with His love and forgiveness, His comfort and compassion, His guidance and direction. As we humbly fall to the ground, God molds and shapes us into the likeness of His Son. As God lifts us up, He makes us into all that we were made to be—a beautiful display of His splendor.

Isaiah 60:21, "Then all your people will be righteous and they will possess the land forever. They are the shoot I have planted, the work of My hands for the display of My splendor."

Lasting Contentment

Worldly riches do not fulfill the deep yearnings of our hearts, and they were never meant to. Only the love of our Heavenly Savior can truly satisfy our longings and meet every need of our soul. He created us in such a way as to find complete and lasting contentment in Him alone. And for that, I am so grateful.

Philippians 4:19, "And my God will meet all your needs according to the riches of His glory in Christ Jesus."

Two-Wheel Faith

At age five, both of my sons, having just had their bicycle training wheels removed, climbed onto their seats, picked up their feet, and before I had a chance to steady them, took off into the wind, never glancing back. They were fearless and enjoyed the freedom of faith more readily than I did. I was older than most kids when I made the transition to a two-wheel bike—I was around eight or nine years old. I had enjoyed the pleasure of roller skating or scootering around with my friends but admired their freedom of zooming around on a two-wheel bicycle.

I remember the day I got my first big-girl bike. There had been an ad in the paper with one for sale and my Mom and Stepdad took me to check it out. It was the bike of my dreams, metallic purple with a white banana seat and streamers hanging from the handlebars. We took the bike home that day and it became mine, all mine. I even got a white, plastic, woven basket to hang from the handlebars. It was adorned with bright, multi-colored daisies, and it was the right size for tucking my dolls safely inside so they could ride around with me. It was perfect.

Now the issue of riding this sparkly creation was a different story. As much as I desired to race around on two wheels like my friends, fear kept me cautiously dependent upon the extra set of small, rattling wheels that were anchored to the sides of my rear tire. With them, I couldn't go quite as fast as everyone else or I might lose my balance. Without them, fear overcame me. But there came a day that the training wheels came off and I was forced to step out (or ride off) in faith. At first, I sat on the seat and kept my feet firmly on the ground; I did that half walking, half pushing thing to propel myself along. Sometime later that day, I bravely lifted my feet and began to pedal. I was shocked and amazed. I wasn't falling, I was moving forward. I was personally experiencing the freedom of two wheels. Days passed, and the more I practiced, the better and braver I got. I was soon riding up and down driveways and going off curbs. I learned to trust the bike beneath me and enjoy the benefits of what I call *"two-wheel faith."* I also learned that the moment I let fear creep back in was the moment I got wobbly and came to a crashing halt. And boy did it hurt!

Life is like this in a quirky sort a way. Fear keeps us from experiencing the freedom that God wants us to enjoy. Fear takes us captive and holds us back from even trying. Fear puts our focus on all the things that can go wrong instead of everything that could go right. Faith, on the other hand, says, "Give it a go, if you don't attempt you'll never know (or grow)." Faith says, "Keep your eyes on God," and, "He'll catch you if you fall." Faith brings freedom, it inspires us to dream, and motivates us to try. Faith encourages us to trust the God who made us and embrace all that He has in store. Faith says, "All things are possible with God by my side." The memory of my purple and white handlebar streamers flowing in the wind is a testament to what can happen when we act in faith.

Two things I'm learning:

Faith over fear equals freedom.

The more I put my faith into practice, the braver I become.

Hebrews 11:1, "Now faith is confidence in what we hope for and assurance about what we do not see."

Jesus

Jesus. A name like no other.

Jesus came.

Jesus died.

Jesus rose.

Jesus lives.

Jesus reigns.

Jesus saves.

Jesus frees.

Jesus redeems.

Jesus loves.

Jesus did, and continues to do it all.

Jesus. A name like no other.

Acts 4:12, "Salvation is found in no one else, for there is no other name under heaven given to mankind by which we must be saved."

Just Fall

If you ever feel that God is distant,

or that His Presence is no longer near,

just fall to your knees,

and you will surely find Him there.

Psalm 27:8, "My heart says of You, 'Seek His face!'

Your face, LORD, I will seek."

Shine Down

Have you ever noticed how flowers turn their pretty little faces to whichever direction the sun is shining from? They seem to love soaking up the warmth, purposefully letting the sun's radiance settle upon them. That's exactly how I feel whenever I hear the verses below read aloud during a church service. I close my eyes, lift my head, and smile as the words are spoken as a blessing over me. I let them settle gently upon me. I take this promising blessing seriously—I want to soak up every bit of it and savor it deep in my soul.

Numbers 6:24-26, "The LORD bless you

and keep you;

[25] the LORD make His face shine on you

and be gracious to you;

[26] the LORD turn His face toward you

and give you peace."

Listening

Lord, help me to hear from you.
To set aside the busyness and step out of the noise.

Help me to silence my own voice, and just listen and receive.
To be still, and wait for You to speak.

To be open and attentive, receptive to your voice.
Open my ears, my mind, and my heart to hear what You would say.

Proverbs 8:34, "Blessed are those who listen to Me, watching daily at

My doors, waiting at My doorway."

His Merciful Standard

Matthew 18:21-22, "Then Peter came to Jesus and asked, 'Lord, how many times shall I forgive my brother or sister who sins against me? Up to seven times?'

²²Jesus answered, 'I tell you, not seven times, but seventy-seven times.'"

When Jesus answered Peter with an astoundingly high figure as the limit for forgiveness, He didn't mean we should literally keep count until we reach that number. He meant our mercy toward each other should be limitless, with His mercy toward us as the gold standard.

If Jesus could forgive me once and continue to forgive me daily, how could I possibly withhold forgiveness from others? I am completely awed at the endless grace that He shows me; I would have given up on me long ago. I thank the Lord that He is God and I am not. I thank the Lord for grace and mercy beyond my harsh standards. I would much rather show others grace according to His merciful standard than He show me grace according to mine. He is good, so very good to me.

Shared Love

I've often seen hummingbirds gather around a sugary, water-filled feeder, sharing nicely, taking turns filling their tiny beaks with the thirst quenching treat. I have also witnessed times when one big greedy bird selfishly chases the others off, keeping all the good stuff for himself. Oftentimes, we're like this with God's love, forgetting there is more than enough to go around; we try to hoard it all for ourselves. But God has an endless supply of love for all to share. The amazing thing about His love is the fact that the more it's shared, the more there is to go around. His love supply endlessly grows, never running out. It is in constant production. We each get *all* His love—He doesn't give out a portion here, and a portion there. He gives it *all* to every one of us. His love is never divided but always multiplied, especially as we share His love with one another.

1 John 4:9-12, "This is how God showed His love among us: He sent His one and only Son into the world that we might live through Him. [10] This is love: not that we loved God, but that He loved us and sent His Son as an atoning sacrifice for our sins. [11] Dear friends, since God so loved us, we also ought to love one another. [12] No one has ever seen God; but if we love one another, God lives in us and His love is made complete in us."

Little Sparrow

It is true, not even a little sparrow falls to the ground outside of our Heavenly Father's notice and care.

As I walked past the open door, out of the corner of my eye, I caught a glimpse of something small moving on the kitchen floor. Upon closer examination, I realized it was a tiny baby bird who had gotten himself lost and found himself in a place he shouldn't be. He was disoriented and couldn't seem to find his way out, so I grabbed a soft towel, gently scooped him up, carried him outside, and placed him safely on the grass near a bush. I watched as he regained his senses and stability, eventually gathering enough strength to hop into the bush. I knew then that he was okay and I could trust he was well enough to be on his own.

If God delights in using people to bring safety and comfort to His tiny creatures, how much more does He delight in using us to reach out beyond ourselves, to bring help, strength, and hope to one another.

God's eye is on the sparrow and His eye is on you and me! Let's join God on His mission of caring and open our eyes to recognize and meet the needs of each other.

Matthew 10:29-31, "Are not two sparrows sold for a penny? Yet not one of them will fall to the ground outside your Father's care. ³⁰ And even the very hairs of your head are all numbered. ³¹ So don't be afraid; you are worth more than many sparrows."

Blessed Exchange

We each go through seasons of plenty and seasons of want. These seasons are opportunities for us to share and receive with each other. In the times when our lives are full and overflowing, we are blessed to help those who lack. When we encounter those same times of need in our own lives, it's our turn to receive and allow others to bless us. This give and take, bless and be blessed exchange can be expressed in so many ways—emotionally, physically, spiritually, practically. When we live this way, the cycle of blessings goes around and round and never runs out. Seasons come and seasons go, but with each other—and Jesus as our bond— we can weather the weather, rain or shine.

Ecclesiastes 4:9-12, "Two are better than one, because they have a good return for their labor: ¹⁰ If either of them falls down, one can help the other up. But pity anyone who falls and has no one to help them up. ¹¹ Also, if two lie down together, they will keep warm. But how can one keep warm alone? ¹² Though one may be overpowered, two can defend themselves. A cord of three strands is not quickly broken."

A Necessity

Meeting with a group of friends on a regular basis for Bible study, prayer, and fellowship may sound like a frivolous luxury, but for me it's a definite necessity. These gatherings hold me accountable, keep me in the Word, and quite honestly, they improve my demeanor, making me an all-around nicer girl. Getting together with like-minded women fills me up with God's goodness which overflows into other areas of my life. God calls us each to journey with Him but also recommends finding companions for our lives. His desire and design is for us to be in community with others who love Him as much as we do. Ask God to lead you to a group or send some special friends your way. Whenever you come together, Jesus will surely be there too.

Matthew 18:20, "For where two or three gather in My name, there am I with them."

Kingdom Girl

Although I was born and raised in sunny Southern California, I must admit that sometimes I feel as if I have a bit of southern country girl hiding inside. I could just as easily run barefoot through the tall cool grass as I could walk along the warm golden sand. I would be happy as a clam sitting on the front porch swing, sipping iced sweet tea, just the same as I would peering out from under the brim of my hat at the rolling waves of the Pacific Ocean. As much as these two locations and states of mind tug at my heart, there is a place above every other that whispers my name and calls me to make it my *home sweet home*. Heaven is this place where I feel perfectly content. Even though at the moment I live here on earth, with Jesus as my Savior, my heart finds its home in His Kingdom, residing contentedly with Him. In the Presence of Jesus is where I run free. I'm completely surrendered, and totally at peace. Jesus and Heaven, there's no better place to be.

I may be a native Californian with a smidgen of southern gal thrown in, but at the root and in my soul, I am a devoted Kingdom girl through and through.

Psalm 145:13, "Your kingdom is an everlasting kingdom, and Your dominion endures through all generations. The LORD is trustworthy in all He promises and faithful in all He does."

Leap of Faith

Imagine that one morning you receive a text from your son informing you that the following weekend he would be willingly jumping out of a perfectly good airplane. Well, this was a reality for me. Since he's an adult there wasn't much I could do or say. The one thing I could do and did do was pray. The day came when my son did jump out, but he was not alone. He was securely strapped to the frame of another. When my son took his leap of faith, it was not based on his own capability, but on the capability of his instructor. My son said that they were so tightly connected they moved as one. Wherever the instructor leaned my son leaned too. When the instructor prepared to exit the plane, my son moved to the edge too; when the instructor leaped out, my son leapt too. The instructor was the one in perfect control—he had the parachute at his command which he released at the precise moment to ensure their safe landing. My son obeyed his instructions and trusted his lead, and I am happy to say he remained scratch-free. He now looks back and recalls the death-defying event with new confidence and joy at what he achieved.

Life calls us into situations that defy all reason. Some days, to simply step out of bed can feel like a leap of faith. But God our Father is also our Heavenly Instructor; when we're strapped tightly to Him, following His lead, listening to His voice, moving as he moves, we too can achieve the impossible. By connecting our lives securely to Him, we can do what we previously had not even dared to dream.

Philippians 4:13, "I can do all this through Him who gives me strength."

Lifeline

Jesus, You are my lifeline. I don't know how people live, much less die, without grabbing hold of the hope You offer. In You, I find my hope for today, tomorrow, and well beyond the grave. In You, I have abundant life now and eternal life forever. Amen.

Psalm 71:14, "As for me, I will always have hope; I will praise You more and more."

Marvelous Creation

You are God's marvelous creation—when you were yet unseen to the world, He was knitting you together in your mother's womb. And to this day He's still weaving you into His precious miracle. Within the depths of your heart, where no one else has ever ventured, He's creating His breathtaking works of wonder. As long as you walk this earth, He continues the profound process of knitting you together and growing you up into the person He desires you to be.

Psalm 139:13-16, "For You created my inmost being; You knit me together in my mother's womb. I praise You because I am fearfully and wonderfully made; Your works are wonderful, I know that full well. ¹⁵ My frame was not hidden from You when I was made in the secret place, when I was woven together in the depths of the earth. ¹⁶ Your eyes saw my unformed body; all the days ordained for me were written in Your book before one of them came to be."

His Follower

Whether I'm tall or short, fat or thin, old or young, black, white, brown, orange, or purple for that matter, my true identity is found within my heart. It's found in my Lord and Savior, my precious Jesus. My appearance is external; my identity internal. I might grow around the middle or shrink in size, I might get age spots and wrinkles, but my heart will forever remain the same— I am a follower of Jesus. That's who I truly am.

John 10:27, "My sheep listen to My voice; I know them, and they follow Me."

Meet You

Lord, forgive me for neglecting time alone with You. Help me to tune my ears to the sound of You calling my name; to surrender my hurry, and stop what I'm doing; to seek a place of seclusion, and meet with You there—face-to-face, in the quiet. Amen.

Exodus 33:11, "The LORD would speak to Moses face to face, as one speaks to a friend."

More Than Popcorn Prayers

I plopped myself onto the couch with bowl of microwave popcorn in hand. I clicked the on T.V. to catch some afternoon news. As is common, the news was filled with heartbreaking stories of death and mayhem and violence and sadness. As I sat there munching on my popcorn, I paused and began praying for the individuals flashing across my screen. They were heartfelt prayers, but I felt the Lord gently remind me that He desires more than just popcorn prayers from me, more than one or two sentence snippets, thrown up in the air. God reminded me that as much as He appreciates those brief encounters, He truly covets the prayers I offer up in quiet, devoted dedication to Him. He asks me to not neglect times of deep prayer, spoken in solitude with Him. I don't need to forsake my quick couch-time prayers, but I do need to integrate many more isolated closet-time devotions. (I literally sit or bow down on the floor of my walk-in closet.)

Matthew 6:6, "But when you pray, go into your room, close the door and pray to your Father, who is unseen. Then your Father, who sees what is done in secret, will reward you."

In Jesus' Name

We can approach God praying our own wants and our own plans, or we can humbly and wisely come to Him, praying for His will and seeking His plans for our lives. When Jesus says *ask whatever we wish in His name and it will be done for us*, it is with the understanding that as His followers, His will has become our will, and we will pray accordingly.

Before praying, pause and consider, *would Jesus really want to sign His name to this prayer? Would He truly endorse this request?* If the answer is "yes," then release it heavenward, send it on its way.

John 15:7, *"If you remain in Me and My words remain in you, ask whatever you wish, and it will be done for you."*

My Refuge

There are times I want to retreat into myself and withdraw from everything. That's precisely the time I need Jesus most. At that point, before running away, it's then that I must choose to run into His arms. It's essential for me to retreat into His refuge, draw near to His Presence, and find my everything in Him.

Psalm 34:8, "Taste and see that the LORD is good; blessed is the one who takes refuge in Him."

On His Behalf

To everyone who believes in the name of Jesus and receives Him as King, to him or her He gives the key to His Kingdom. He entrusts His citizens with the greatest responsibility under heaven. He not only grants us entrance into His Glorious Kingdom, but He also instructs us to invite others to enter as well. Our role is not to stand at the gates as an obstacle for others to climb over; we are not the Kingdom bouncers choosing only the most desirable to enter in based on our criteria. The Kingdom of Heaven is not an exclusive club, it's an all-inclusive family. The only thing needed to gain entrance is *Jesus*. He invites us all. Our responsibility is to personally accept His invitation and then hold the door open and celebrate as others enter too.

As holders of the key, we are Christ's ambassadors, extending the invitation of reconciliation to all and welcoming all who accept to take their place in God's Kingdom. We are called to use our key in the name of Jesus and in the nature of His love, grace, and mercy.

2 Corinthians 5:20, "We are therefore Christ's ambassadors, as though God were making His appeal through us. We implore you on Christ's behalf: Be reconciled to God."

My Treasure

Jesus challenges us to take a good hard look at our treasures—the things we value most—because whatever they may be, that is where we'll find our heart. Are our heart and our hope set on the pursuit of an earthly treasure that doesn't have lasting value or any true power? Or is it set on Jesus and the heavenly riches He has promised us? His is a treasure that lasts forever, offers us saving hope, and has the power to change our lives.

Matthew 6:21, "For where your treasure is, there your heart will be also."

Pure Fruit

Fruit is the natural outflowing of what has been put into my life—either good, or bad. A life full of sin is a life full of angst, bearing fruit of shame and regret. A life filled with the righteousness of Christ is a life bearing fruit of His blessed peace, peace in knowing I am made right with my Savior and am pleasing in the eyes of my Lord. The peace I feel inside can't help but show as the change in my demeanor starts to blossom and overflow. A new, quiet calm and a settled assurance are the fruit my life yields as I pursue Jesus and embark with Him in the holy way of righteousness. My pure fruit of peace is a testament to the honor and glory of God.

Isaiah 32:17, "The fruit of that righteousness will be peace; its effect will be quietness and confidence forever."

Out it Goes

In His love, Jesus invites us, welcomes us, and receives us just as we are. In His love, He also begins the work of transforming our lives into something much better, something that represents Him well. As we begin anew with Him, some things no longer fit or have a place in our lives—things such as gossip, hatred, bitterness, unforgiveness, rage, envy, bad habits, foul language. Jesus looks at each of these behaviors and says, "out it goes." Getting rid of the old makes room for the new, giving attitudes such as righteousness, holiness, goodness, and purity a clean heart and plenty of space in which to flourish. So, when Jesus decides to purge something out of your life, remind yourself of the abundant blessings that will flow, then agree with Him and say, "out it goes."

Ephesians 4:30-32, "And do not grieve the Holy Spirit of God, with whom you were sealed for the day of redemption. [31] Get rid of all bitterness, rage and anger, brawling and slander, along with every form of malice. [32] Be kind and compassionate to one another, forgiving each other, just as in Christ God forgave you."

Don't Worry

Concerns in life are only natural, often based on real problems that need rational solutions. Worries on the other hand are based on unnatural, irrational fears of "what if's" that may never materialize. Worries are blown-up versions of our simple concerns. Worries are paralyzing. They cause us to expend our energies on replaying harmful, negative thoughts over and over while keeping us from moving forward or accomplishing anything of measure.

Turning our concerns over to God before they grow into worries yields much greater results. Placing our worries into God's capable hands frees us up to work with Him in productively addressing matters. His power accomplishes infinitely more than we can imagine and do on our own. His power moves mole hills, and it moves mountains too. So, give God your concerns before they become worries. And if you find yourself taking them back into your own hands, keep handing them over for as long as it takes till you finally and fully surrender them into His care.

Matthew 6:27, "Can any one of you by worrying add a single hour to your life?"

Matthew 6:33-34, "But seek first His kingdom and His righteousness, and all these things will be given to you as well. [34] Therefore do not worry about tomorrow, for tomorrow will worry about itself. Each day has enough trouble of its own."

Set Free

In Jesus, we are no longer captive to worry, doubt, and fear—in His name we are set free. Shackles of shame, bitterness, and anger have no more claim on our hearts. Jesus has unlocked the door. He holds the key. He has indeed set us free. Far too often though, we forget our freedom and we live as though it isn't so. Jesus warns us not to fall back into bondage to things that no longer have a hold on or place in our lives. He paid the highest price to release us, so let's remember that and daily live *set free*.

Galatians 5:1, "It is for freedom that Christ has set us free. Stand firm, then, and do not let yourselves be burdened again by a yoke of slavery."

Perfect Prescription

I have the perfect prescription for you: whenever you're feeling down in the dumps, or over-loaded and overwhelmed, take a step outside with Jesus! At times like this, a change of environment, a fresh perspective, and time with Jesus are just what the doctor orders. I can personally testify to the benefits of this simple remedy.

If you're not able to get around that well, just grab a seat on the porch and take in the view. If your body allows, put on your walking shoes and head around the block. I guarantee a lift in your mood and a healing in your heart. You'd have to be pretty determined to stay *stuck in your funk* for the change in surroundings to not affect your mood. Once outside, the glorious sunshine will warm your soul; the same breeze that gently rustles through the branches will sweep through and clear your mind of clutter; the playlist of the chirping birds will put a new song in your heart; the dream-like puffy clouds will draw your gaze heavenward, shining new hope into your eyes; the scent of blooming flowers will overwhelm your senses, transporting you to a place of contented rest.

I fully understand this may be easier to do in California and in summertime than in other places and other seasons, but regardless, there is always beauty to be found (even snow, rain, and fog reveal the Hand of the Creator) just outside your door. The scenery can even be captured and appreciated through your window from the snuggly warmth inside. In allowing your gaze to wander and ponder the outdoors, you experience a much-needed respite away from the burdens weighing heavy on your mind. Here you find time to pause, reflect, rest, breathe deeply, and pray to the Lord. And when it's time to return your focus back inside, to the place you call home, it will be with the blessed calm of a settled soul.

Psalm 62:5, "Yes, my soul, find rest in God; my hope comes from Him."

Simply Follow

This world is complicated. Relationships, politics, health, finances, you name it, it's probably complicated. In the midst of all this complexity, my heart seeks simplicity, plain and simple. The last thing I want is for my faith to be complicated, and fortunately, Jesus has simplified it perfectly. He has stripped away all the rule following, done away with all the works-based religions. He tells us, "Forget about keeping your checklist of do's and don'ts. Just follow My example, I'll show you how to live. Wake up every morning and seek My face; lay down each night and praise My Name. Walk the path before you by following My lead; endure the storm around you by hanging onto on Me. Love the people around you by loving in My Name."

Faith is simply Jesus.

Simply seek and follow Him. He uncomplicates the rest.

Matthew 16:24, "Then Jesus said to His disciples, 'Whoever wants to be My disciple must deny themselves and take up their cross and follow Me.'"

A Simple Equation

If you're anything like me, mathematical word equations were your least favorite assignment in school. Problems such as: If the bus drove 57 miles, at 42 mph, with 107 people on board, making 13 stops along the way, what time would the bus arrive at its destination? Dumb-founded, staring at this problem, I would think, *If I were on the bus I would just ask the driver for an estimation.* Fortunately, the equations the Lord gives us are much simpler, easier to understand, and I actually care about the answer—which He clearly spells out for us in His Word. The Bible is our study guide and solution manual, all wrapped up in one.

One of my favorite equations in the Bible is: Love=Hope=Joy

You see, once we comprehend the lavish love that God has for us, our hearts become filled with hope. Once we latch onto the hope we have in the Lord, our lives explode with joy. Joy then can't help but overflow to everyone around.

A simple equation—the kind I like!

P.S. Don't try solving my bus math problem. I made it up and there is no answer.

Ephesians 3:17-18, "So that Christ may dwell in your hearts through faith. And I pray that you, being rooted and established in love, [18] may have power, together with all the Lord's holy people, to grasp how wide and long and high and deep is the love of Christ..."

Possible Adventures

Life is what we make of it. Far too often we have the idea that adventure is only found on a grand scale, so we intently focus, schedule, and plan for the big event. And in the process, we miss out on the small everyday adventures right outside our door. We may even drive right past opportunities that are calling us to explore.

My son is one who notices and heeds any chance for exploration. One year as his birthday approached, we discussed options for an upcoming party—pizza, bowling, laser tag, backyard, etc. Despite all these exciting possibilities, he chose to have an afternoon at "the dirt track." It was actually a large vacant lot situated beside the highway. We drove past it all the time, and often we would see motorized dirt bikes riding along the trails and jumping over small hills. Where we saw dirt, my son saw potential. So the day of his celebration, my husband and I loaded two small bicycles into the back of our truck—our son's and his best friend's. Shortly after arriving at our destination, the two of them eagerly set off, their little legs pumping hard, the dust flying as their wheels spun propelling them onward. In this small adventure, their world grew big as the path unfolded before them.

Of course, we want to enjoy the thrill of the big escapades, but we don't want to forsake the pleasure of the smaller adventures that are waiting to be discovered and appreciated right under our nose—they can be exhilarating too.

Let's ask God to give us a keen eye for exploration, a youthful mind of appreciation, and an overall sense of wonder, to notice and take advantage of the many possible adventures right around us.

Psalm 65:8, "The whole earth is filled with awe at Your wonders; where morning dawns, where evening fades, You call forth songs of joy."

Rescuing Love

God's love is a rescuing love sent directly from Heaven in the form of His Son. God's love rescues us daily from the grip of sin, eternally saves us from the power of death. His love removes our condemnation through the sacrifice of Jesus. His love accomplished what our hard work could not. No matter how hard we tried, we could never save ourselves; a rescuer was necessary for any hope of being set free. Jesus is our Rescuer, our Savior sent from above. He rescues all who believe and ask.

John 3:16, "For God so loved the world that He gave His one and only Son, that whoever believes in Him shall not perish but have eternal life."

Out of Gratitude

We worship, surrender, and seek God not for what we want Him to do, but because of what He's already done. We bow our knees and lift our hearts before Him out of gratitude for His gift of salvation and eternal life, and every blessing He's poured out.

Psalm 16:11, "You make known to me the path of life; You will fill me with joy in Your presence, with eternal pleasures at Your right hand."

Say Jesus

When you find yourself fumbling and struggling to find the right words, just say "Jesus." His Name is the Almighty Answer to every situation, every need, every desire. Calling His Name brings much needed help. Singing His Name fills the air and our hearts with joyful praise. Speaking His Name brings light to the darkness. Claiming His Name releases great power and strength. Clinging to His Name ushers in calming peace and reassuring hope. When at a loss for words, simply say "Jesus."

Philippians 2:10-11, "That at the name of Jesus every knee should bow, in heaven and on earth and under the earth, and every tongue acknowledge that Jesus Christ is Lord, to the glory of God the Father."

Seeking You, Lord

Lord, as much as our world and our nation need Your healing touch, our individual lives need You desperately so. You promise that in humbling ourselves and seeking Your face, our healing is found.

So begin with me, Lord. I'm seeking you and laying down my pride. I look to You with humility and hope, asking You to mend my heart, purify and cleanse my mind. Restore and redeem all that is broken in me. Magnify Your Name by performing miracles only You can perform—only You can heal the depths of a soul and repair our land as a whole.

2 Chronicles 7:14, "if My people, who are called by My name, will humble themselves and pray and seek My face and turn from their wicked ways, then I will hear from heaven, and I will forgive their sin and will heal their land."

Eagerly Exchange

To possess hope in the present and for the future, we must first let God repossess our past—our past sins, hurts, regrets, fears, and insecurities. If we truly understood the hope He holds out for us, we would be more than willing—in fact we would be jumping at the chance—to hand over the pain, shame, and bitterness that loom over us. We would eagerly exchange the junk that too often holds us in bondage for the freedom He so generously offers. It's time to give God our past and grab hold of the hope and the future He intends for us to have.

Proverbs 23:18, "There is surely a future hope for you, and your hope will not be cut off."

Word of Hope

Far too often we look for hope and the answers to life in all the wrong places. We grab every self-help book on the market, heed the advice of every well-meaning friend, and even watch afternoon television therapists hoping to find what our hearts are longing for. All this searching and grasping will leave us just as empty as before unless it leads us to Jesus. So instead of rushing here and there looking for answers, searching for some inspiration of hope, let's stop, be still, and wait on the Lord. The wisest thing we can do is turn to Him, place our hope in Him and invite Him to speak His Word of life into our situation. God's Word is abounding with the hope we so desperately need because it points us to Him. Let God be your lifeline of hope. Open your Bible and then bow your head in prayer. Tell God you believe and place your hope in what His Word says. Then wait for Him to speak personally to you.

Psalm 130:5, "I wait for the LORD, my whole being waits, and in His Word I put my hope."

Survival Kit

Years ago, fanny packs (little pouches people strap around their waists) were all the rage. Although they are no longer considered fashionable, I still choose to wear one every time I go hiking. My fanny pack is black, and roomy enough to hold the many supplies I may need while on the trails. If you peeked inside at the contents, you would most likely find a small tube of sunscreen for reapplication in times of intense sunshine, used to keep me from getting burned. You would come across a pretty, pink, and very sharp pocket knife which could be used to cut myself free from potential danger. You would also find a small bottle of pepper spray, to be used in encounters with dangerous enemies of various sorts—snakes, mountain lions, and the human kind. There is always a water bottle included to keep me refreshed along my journey and a granola bar in case I get hungry. Lastly, a cell phone is always tucked neatly inside so in case of emergency I can call for help immediately.

I realize this is a strange comparison, but, just as my fanny pack holds my makeshift survival kit, The Bible is my real survival kit, not just for the trails, but for everywhere the path of life takes me. This survival kit is available to all.

The Word of God shields us when it feels as if the heat is turned up and we're faced with daily stresses and pressures or up against trials and tribulations.

The Word of God is used to cut us free from the entanglements of sin, shame, bitterness, fear, hatred, anxiety, and more.

The Word of God prepares and equips us to fight off the enemy and the lies that Satan feeds us by teaching us who God is, who we are, and what truth is.

The Word of God refreshes our soul and invigorates us so we can keep moving onward.

The Word of God nourishes and sustains us.

The Word of God directs us to our Savior, our Lifeline in times of emergency, and our Companion for the journey.

The Word of God is our everyday essential survival kit.

Psalm 18:30, "As for God, His way is perfect: The LORD's Word is flawless; He shields all who take refuge in Him."

Sweet Reminders

That first glimmer of light shining brightly against the dark sky compels me in childlike wonder to cast my wishes upward. But as is the case with my dandelion wishes, my wishes upon stars quickly transform into prayers. What begins as a recitation of a wistful children's poem transitions into a heartfelt conversation with my Father. I look up to the sky, picturing Him enthroned in the glory of Heaven, mighty and powerful, with the world at His command, all the while knowing how personally and tenderly He loves me. This drastic contrast of God's strength and gentleness comforts me as nothing else can. Knowing that God has time for me, that He cares about my feelings, that He sees my needs, and that He has the power to act on my behalf gives me unimaginable hope and peace.

Dandelions and stars do not have power, but they can be sweet reminders of my Heavenly Father who does.

Revelation 8:4, "The smoke of the incense, together with the prayers of God's people, went up before God from the angel's hand."

With You Always

As odd as it may seem, there are times we can be in the middle of a crowded room, surrounded by people, and still feel all alone. There are moments, though encircled by family and friends when we encounter isolating loneliness. In these times and in these places, Jesus will meet us. He understands what we feel because He experienced it to the extreme. But as Jesus walked this earth, He relied on the Father and continually drew close to Him. Those times we find ourselves all alone in a crowd, we can believe that Jesus is standing right beside us because He really is there. He is with us in our loneliness. He says, "I am with you always my child, you are never alone."

Matthew 28:20, "and teaching them to obey everything I have commanded you. And surely, I am with you always, to the very end of the age."

Take My Hand

Lord, take my hand and lead me to the Promised Land, the land where your love is the Law by which everything is governed. Lead me to the Land where You reign supreme, where Your justice rules in righteous perfection.

Lord, take my hand and lead me to the place of hope fulfilled and faith completed. Lead me to that place of contentment and joy overflowing. Lead me to the place my heart longs for, the place of Your Holy Presence, the place of eternal fellowship with You.

Lord, take me to the Promised Land, where my soul finds peaceful rest in my realized inheritance.

Leviticus 20:24, "But I said to you, 'You will possess their land; I will give it to you as an inheritance, a land flowing with milk and honey.'

I am the LORD your God, who has set you apart from the nations."

The Shepherd

Luke 15:3-7, "Then Jesus told them this parable: [4] 'Suppose one of you has a hundred sheep and loses one of them. Doesn't he leave the ninety-nine in the open country and go after the lost sheep until he finds it? [5] And when he finds it, he joyfully puts it on his shoulders [6] and goes home. Then he calls his friends and neighbors together and says, "Rejoice with me; I have found my lost sheep." [7] I tell you that in the same way there will be more rejoicing in heaven over one sinner who repents than over ninety-nine righteous persons who do not need to repent.'"

The star of the preceding parable is the Shepherd, not the lost sheep. Every story in the Bible revolves around God highlighting His love, His power, His mercy, and grace. Most of all, they emphasize His resolve to bring us back. Jesus is The Good Shepherd, and as His sheep, He knows us each by name. He intimately cares about us individually and wants not even one of us to be lost. In our times of wandering, He seeks us, He finds us. He lifts us up and, laying our weary bodies across His strong shoulders, carries us home, to the safety of His fold. The joy of our return sparks a contagious celebration, resounding throughout all of Heaven.

The Father

Luke 15:20-24, "So he got up and went to his father. But while he was still a long way off, his father saw him and was filled with compassion for him; he ran to his son, threw his arms around him and kissed him. ²¹ The son said to him, 'Father, I have sinned against heaven and against you. I am no longer worthy to be called your son.' ²² But the father said to his servants, 'Quick! Bring the best robe and put it on him. Put a ring on his finger and sandals on his feet. ²³ Bring the fattened calf and kill it. Let's have a feast and celebrate. ²⁴ For this son of mine was dead and is alive again; he was lost and is found.' So they began to celebrate.'"

In this Parable that Jesus told, we find the beautiful message of redemption.

The son's role in his own redemption was simply to repent of his ways and return to his father.

The father's part in redemption was to let his son choose, fail on his own, and finally come to the end of himself. The father's part was mercy and grace, watching and waiting, reaching out and embracing, accepting and forgiving. The father clothed his son with dignity, restored him to honor, and fed his every need. The father's part was rejoicing and celebrating and welcoming his child home.

This story clearly represents our own—our rebellion, our awakening, and our Father's lavish grace towards us.

In our story, we receive all the mercy, and God gets all the glory!

The Coin

Luke 15:8-10, "Or suppose a woman has ten silver coins and loses one. Doesn't she light a lamp, sweep the house and search carefully until she finds it?[9] And when she finds it, she calls her friends and neighbors together and says, 'Rejoice with me; I have found my lost coin.'[10] In the same way, I tell you, there is rejoicing in the presence of the angels of God over one sinner who repents."

In the stories Jesus told:

The sheep slowly wandered away until he lost sight of his shepherd and suddenly found himself all alone.

The son chose to leave and travel away from his father to a place so foreign and distant from his home.

The coin neither wandered, nor left on its own; it was simply lost, maybe through no fault of its own.

We, like the sheep, often wander from our Jesus. Like the son, we willfully separate ourselves from our Father. Other times though, like the coin, we are quite simply lost. Possibly it's because we've never heard the Gospel message. Maybe no one has ever taken the time to tell us about Jesus and His love and His hope. But, the Lord will not let us stay lost. In His mercy, He will not stop searching until He recovers our hearts. He is the Light that shines in the darkest of places. His love sweeps every crevice and corner in which we could hide, and when He finds us, He'll call all of Heaven together to celebrate His treasured prize.

The Hope

The hope of Jesus is never out of reach; His arms are outstretched wide for you and me.

The hope of Jesus never tires; it is constant and continuous. It is fresh every day.

The hope of Jesus is never outgrown; His hope is for every age, from the very young to the weary old.

The hope of Jesus is perfectly suited to every occasion; whatever the circumstance, His hope is custom made to order.

The hope of Jesus is just the right size; His hope fits all our needs—the overwhelmingly big and insignificantly small.

The hope of Jesus is what our hearts require; His hope fills in the gaps, making us whole.

Psalm 33:21-22, "In Him our hearts rejoice,

for we trust in His holy name.

²² May Your unfailing love be with us, LORD,

even as we put our hope in You."

Thriving

As I sit here at the doctor's office filling in the blanks on my health record, my identity is reduced to a few simple questions and answers—*name, age, weight, height, birthdate, my health history and that of my family members*. When I come to the space asking my *race*, for some reason I find it funny, and I'm tempted to write "human." I fill out these same papers year after year. Although this information reveals a bit about my health, to see my truest condition and how well I'm thriving, you must look at my relationship with Jesus. To really thrive and not merely survive, my life must remain connected to Him. The questions to be asked should be, "Are you getting a daily dose of your Savior? Are you seeking Him regularly, encountering Him in prayer, soaking in His Presence, and digging into His Word?" The condition of my health depends greatly on my answers to these insightful and revealing questions. Only by continually securing my life to His do I remain strong, healthy, growing, and thriving.

John 15:5, "I am the vine; you are the branches. If you remain in Me and I in you, you will bear much fruit; apart from Me you can do nothing."

True Joy

True joy is a treasure Jesus offers us, more priceless than pure gold. It is not found in our external circumstances which change like the shifting sand constantly blown and formed at the whim of the wind. True joy is found only in Jesus. He is always steady and unfailingly sure. True joy is discovered when we allow Jesus to make a glorious change in our perspective. When we begin to see life as Jesus sees it and find our contentment in Him, only then will true joy settle into our soul.

True joy, like hope and faith, is also a mindset we must choose to make our own by purposefully grabbing hold of Jesus and letting Him grab hold of our soul. True joy can't be kept quiet; it overflows and sings aloud. Others will hear our joy-filled song and acknowledge it must come from Jesus.

Psalm 126:2, "Our mouths were filled with laughter, our tongues with songs of joy. Then it was said among the nations, 'The LORD has done great things for them.'"

Two Fish

As a young girl, my Dad and I made many Saturday afternoon trips to the pet shop. We usually walked the aisles admiring the wide variety of possible pets, but this one afternoon we left the store with a bagful of goldfish—ten fish to be exact. We brought them home to my grandparents' house and released them into the swimming pool in the backyard. Let me take a moment to explain the state of their swimming pool. Years before, it had been damaged in a large earthquake and had remained unused and unmaintained ever since. Green algae were growing so plentifully you could no longer see beneath the murky surface. The fish fed on the algae and the occasional bread scraps we threw their way. Not long after their release into this enormous fish pond, the ten-tiny goldfish began multiplying and growing beyond anything we had expected. We would catch glimpses of them whenever they came up to feed. Soon, there seemed to be hundreds, if not thousands of very large fish residing in my grandparents' pool.

This silly story reminds me of the incredibly miraculous and much more profound story of Jesus and His multiplying fish and loaves.

Many thousands of people followed Jesus as He traveled near the Sea of Galilee. Some were hungry to hear His words, others sought to experience His healing, and still others were just plain curious or merely going along with the crowd. This one particular day, they all gathered close to catch a glimpse of this mysterious Man, to hear what He would say and see what He would do. They lingered long into the afternoon not wanting to leave for fear of missing anything. Having not eaten all day, they probably had empty and rumbling stomachs. Knowing this, Jesus told His disciples to have the people sit down and prepare to eat.

From among the crowd, a young boy emerged, and selflessly donated his two fish and five loaves of bread. This small boy with big faith gave all he had to Jesus, and Jesus greatly multiplied the meager offerings into something grand. Jesus took the two fish and five loaves of bread and fed more than 5,000 people, till all were full and satisfied as if they had just eaten an extravagant Thanksgiving spread. Even after everyone had eaten their fill, leftovers literally overflowed from the baskets, reminding us that there is always an abundance with Jesus.

Whatever we bring to Jesus He transforms into something amazing. Bring Him our praise, He'll fill us with joy; bring Him our heartache, He'll fill us with hope; bring Him our uncertainties, He'll show us the way; bring Him our worries, He'll calm our fears. We bring what we have, offer it all to Jesus, empty ourselves out before Him, and He fills us up. He nourishes our souls with an abundance we've never known before. When we bring our "two fish" to Jesus, He multiplies them beyond our expectations.

John 6: 9-13, "'Here is a boy with five small barley loaves and two small fish, but how far will they go among so many?' ¹⁰Jesus said, 'Have the people sit down.' There was plenty of grass in that place, and they sat down (about five thousand men were there)."Jesus then took the loaves, gave thanks, and distributed to those who were seated as much as they wanted. He did the same with the fish.¹²When they had all had enough to eat, He said to His disciples, 'Gather the pieces that are left over. Let nothing be wasted.' ¹³So they gathered them and filled twelve baskets with the pieces of the five barley loaves left over by those who had eaten."

Unswerving

Faith is not something we can put on a back burner or place up on a shelf. Faith is meant to be kept not just within reach for those dire hours of need, but instilled right in our hearts, inspiring hope in whatever the moment brings. Faith is to be chosen and put into action everyday of our lives—there's never a day to be skipped. Faith firmly placed in the faithfulness of our Good Lord above fills us with heavenly, unswerving hope for this world below.

Tuck a reserve of faith in your heart, cling tightly to the hope of God today, and be prepared no matter what dreaded disruption or joy-filled occasion comes your way.

Hebrews 10:23, "Let us hold unswervingly to the hope we profess,

for He who promised is faithful."

Understood

Those days when you feel completely misunderstood, when your words come out all wrong and your actions seem awkwardly strange, when your emotions are all jumbled up inside, and even you have a hard time understanding yourself, there is One who completely understands. The thoughts you can't find words for, God already knows. The actions you grasp to find explanation for need no explaining to your Father above. Hand Him your heart, your thoughts, and emotions; He'll unscramble them all. In His Presence, you are fully understood, and with His help, you'll begin to understand yourself when you see "you" through His eyes.

Psalm 139:2, "You know when I sit and when I rise; You perceive my thoughts from afar."

So Close

In your sorrow, in the midst of heartache, turn to God for your comfort and strength. Seek Jesus for your solace and peace. He knows your sadness and feels your pain. He empathizes with your difficulties. There is nothing you are going through that He does not understand. He's witnessed loved ones die. He's faced temptation of every kind and overcome each time. He's experienced rejection to the ultimate extent. He enters in with you and comforts as no one else so fully can. Come to Him, let His arms envelope you in a warm embrace. Lay your head on His shoulder and let your tears fall. Listen to Him tenderly speak your name; hear His gentle words of encouragement tailored especially for you. When your spirit is crushed, grab hold of His hand. He's closer than you think.

Psalm 34:18, "The LORD is close to the brokenhearted and saves those who are crushed in spirit."

Watches Over

Day and night, the LORD vigilantly watches over my life. The Creator of heaven, the One who keeps the earth spinning, takes notice of me. What an awe-inspiring revelation, that from high on His throne, He sees my cares, He knows my concerns, He watches over me daily. While I sleep, He does not rest. As I walk, He steadies my feet on His stable path. Any hardships I face, I know without a doubt that He has my back. Even though He has universe upon universe under His command, He takes notice of me. I am awed by the fact that my life is constantly under His loving and watchful eye, not just today, but tomorrow and forever.

Psalm 121:1-8, "I lift up my eyes to the mountains— where does my help come from? ²My help comes from the LORD, the Maker of heaven and earth. ³He will not let your foot slip— He who watches over you will not slumber; ⁴indeed, He who watches over Israel will neither slumber nor sleep.

⁵The LORD watches over you— the LORD is your shade at your right hand; ⁶the sun will not harm you by day, nor the moon by night. ⁷The LORD will keep you from all harm— He will watch over your life; ⁸the LORD will watch over your coming and going both now and forevermore."

Your Gravity

Wherever I am, Lord, the gravity of Your love draws me near to You. It calls my name and tugs at my heart. The gravity of Your love is a force unlike any other; I cannot resist its pull, nor do I even want to try. The gravity of Your love draws me in and anchors my soul. In Your love, Lord, my feet find solid ground on which to stand, and my heart finds hope on which to soar.

Song of Songs 7:10, "I belong to my beloved, and his desire is for me."

Thankful

Pause, reflect, appreciate, give thanks. Thanksgiving is a day set aside for just such an occasion. The whirling and rushing that usually distract our attention and steal our notice of everyday blessings are put on hold with the specific purpose of counting these often-overlooked gifts. A whole day for rejoicing, celebrating, and giving thanks—thanks to our Father in Heaven, the giver of all good gifts. Every blessing we have comes directly from His loving hand, straight from His merciful heart.

Giving thanks warms the heart and encourages the mind as we redirect our thoughts onto the presence of His goodness in our daily lives. Let's have a heart full of thanks on this special day and carry it with us into all the days to come.

Psalm 100:4, "Enter His gates with thanksgiving and His courts with praise; give thanks to Him and praise His name."

Christmas To-Do List

1. Celebrate Jesus
2. Show love
3. Show kindness
4. Give smiles
5. Give hugs
6. Give encouraging words
7. Slow down
8. Appreciate time with loved ones
9. Make memories
10. Bless others

Ephesians 5:1-2, "Follow God's example, therefore, as dearly loved children [2] and walk in the way of love, just as Christ loved us and gave Himself up for us as a fragrant offering and sacrifice to God."

Indescribable Gift

The love, mercy, grace, power, and justice of God are all wrapped up in One Beautiful Gift—The Gift of Jesus our Savior, Jesus our Lord. God's Gift brings us salvation and freedom. His Gift grants us peace, hope, and joy. God's Gift of His very own Son is a lavish demonstration of His enormous love for us, a love that goes beyond the greatest extent and farthest length, all to draw us near to Him and make us each His child. God's gift brings us a sure hope we can cling to for now and all of eternity.

Open His Gift and receive His abundant love today! It's the best Gift you'll ever receive!

2 Corinthians 9:15, "Thanks be to God for His indescribable Gift."

Hope Fulfilled

As the flying scraps of gift-wrapping begin to settle and the seasonal hustle and bustle calms to a breathable pace, I allow myself a few moments to sit, reflect, and savor the recent festivities. Last night as I was heading off to bed, first stopping to unplug the Christmas tree lights, the lure of quiet and solitude whispered my name and beckoned me to sit for a spell. As I plopped myself down on the couch I recalled the abundant celebrations that had only just passed in this most joyous of seasons; a season punctuated with parties, gifts, decorations, and lights, with gatherings and reunions of family and friends; a season punctuated with the sounds of laughter and chatter, and the taste of indulgent goodies galore. As I sit here in quiet contemplation, my gaze wanders over the beautifully decorated tree before me, and as my eyes pause on each ornament, memories come to mind. A newly received ornament catches my full attention as it rests on the branches at the center of the tree. Within its beautiful rectangular shaped glass with gilded silver edges is a picture highlighting the journey of the Three Wise Men. These men of the Bible had heard the promises of God and believed them to be true. They clung to the hope that God would provide a Savior, that God would send a King unlike any other— a King of truth, justice, love, mercy, holiness, peace, and perfection. The *wise men* knew to be on the lookout for the heavenly sign of a special, God-designated star which would lead them to a place of hope fulfilled. Believing the promises of God, the men traveled from a far-off country, following the star until it came to rest above the house where their long-awaited Savior resided. They brought gifts of great worth—gold, frankincense, and myrrh— in worship of this highly-anticipated Newborn King.

Even now all signs and arrows point the way to Jesus, if only our hearts will follow. Jesus is the One in whom all our hope is fulfilled. And when we find Him, we too offer Him our best gift. We surrender all we have—our hearts, our lives, our worship, our praise—laying them at His feet.

Finding Jesus is our hope fulfilled.

Matthew 2:1-12, "After Jesus was born in Bethlehem in Judea, during the time of King Herod, Magi from the east came to Jerusalem ² and asked, 'Where is the one who has been born king of the Jews? We saw his star when it rose and have come to worship him.'

³ When King Herod heard this he was disturbed, and all Jerusalem with him. ⁴ When he had called together all the people's chief priests and teachers of the law, he asked them where the Messiah was to be born.⁵ 'In Bethlehem in Judea,' they replied, 'for this is what the prophet has written:

⁶ "But you, Bethlehem, in the land of Judah, are by no means least among the rulers of Judah; for out of you will come a ruler who will shepherd My people Israel."'

⁷ Then Herod called the Magi secretly and found out from them the exact time the star had appeared. ⁸ He sent them to Bethlehem and said, 'Go and search carefully for the Child. As soon as you find Him, report to me, so that I too may go and worship him.'

⁹ After they had heard the king, they went on their way, and the star they had seen when it rose went ahead of them until it stopped over the place where the Child was. ¹⁰ When they saw the star, they were overjoyed. ¹¹ On coming to the house, they saw the Child with His mother Mary, and they bowed down and worshiped Him. Then they opened their treasures and presented Him with gifts of gold, frankincense, and myrrh. ¹² And having been warned in a dream not to go back to Herod, they returned to their country by another route."

Joyfully Sing

I awoke on this day, the very last day of the year, to the sound of excited chatter abounding from the trees surrounding my yard. Cheery little birds greeted the day with song, filling the air with joy and exuberance, as they so often do. They seemed to care not whether it was the last or the first day on the calendar. Their celebration rings in every day; they seem to rejoice at their current blessings and at the promise each day holds.

As the year draws to a close, whatever blessings you recount, whatever possibilities you hope for in the new year, don't lose sight of them or let them fall by the wayside after just a few short days or weeks. Continue to count and recount your blessings and continue to cling to possibility and hope found in each new day. Continue to rejoice and celebrate the coming of dawn. Praise the One who blesses you and seek the One who holds your hope. And like the birds, greet each day with a song in your heart.

Psalm 145:7, "They celebrate Your abundant goodness and joyfully sing of Your righteousness."

Permission Slip

While looking at the pages of my calendar for the upcoming week there appeared to be scarcely little opportunity for quiet, rest, and dedicated time with the Lord. Just coming out of the holiday season and the busyness that entails and the pressing responsibilities looming on the immediate horizon, I longed for just a little time to reconnect with the Lord—to dig deep into His Presence for refreshment and an anchoring of my soul. Well, just as this longing seemed out of reach, God in His goodness intervened and opened my schedule, though not in a way I would have chosen. My body succumbed to a bad cold, requiring me to cancel and reschedule the very things that filled my calendar and crowded out precious time with God. A cold is not usually considered a good thing, but when I let it, it can be used for a very good purpose—a permission slip to be excused from busyness, to sit in quiet, mandated rest with my Savior. As He goes to work healing my body, He is also at work revitalizing my soul.

Malachi 4:2, "But for you who revere My name, the sun of righteousness will rise with healing in its rays. And you will go out and frolic like well-fed calves."

Tad Bits of Hope, by You

Tad Bits of Hope, by You

Tad Bits of Hope, by You

Tad Bits of Hope, by You

Tad Bits of Hope, by You

Tad Bits of Hope, by You

Tad Bits of Hope, by You

Tad Bits of Hope, by You

Special Thanks

To Russell, for your love and support all these years. You mean the world to me.

To Camden, for wrapping my words in your beautiful cover design. It's exactly what I hoped for, and makes my heart happy.

To Mackenzie, for taking the time to review this little book of mine. You are so dear to me.

To Christian, for your continuous encouragement and skillful editing. You refined my words so poetically.

To Jesus, of course, the constant source of all my hope.

Getting to Know the Author

First and foremost, I am a woman who loves the Lord with all her heart. I am married to a wonderful man, and I'm a mother of two young men (who used to be small). I am a daughter, a sister, a friend, a neighbor. I have a dog, I enjoy taking walks outside, and I like chips and salsa. I serve in the women's ministry at my local church in Westlake Village, California. I enjoy speaking at Teen Challenge and other various women's events. I have a passion for helping women deepen their relationship with Jesus and discover their identity as a child of God through the study of His Word. Although you and I may have different likes or dislikes, relationships or roles, I'm sure many of my life stories can be related to whatever you have going on. I truly thank you for joining me on this journey and hope that you find some encouragement as we walk together with the LORD.

My titles available on Amazon:

A Daughter of the King: Gaining Confidence as a Child of God

Lilies and Lemonade: Joy-Filled Devotions

Promise and Possibilities: Hope-Filled Devotions

You can connect with me on Facebook at: facebook.com/tracyhillauthor

Follow my blog at: tracy-considerthelilies.blogspot.com

Made in the USA
San Bernardino, CA
29 October 2017